Ten P...
about Gr...

ex libris

Candlestick Press

Published by:
Candlestick Press,
Diversity House, 72 Nottingham Road, Arnold, Nottingham UK NG5 6LF
www.candlestickpress.co.uk

Design and typesetting by Diversity Creative Marketing Solutions Ltd.,
www.diversity.agency

Printed by Ratcliff & Roper Print Group, Nottinghamshire, UK

Selection and Introduction © Liz Soar, 2017

Cover illustration © Kathy Morgan
kathymorganart.webplus.net

Candlestick Press monogram © Barbara Shaw, 2008

© Candlestick Press, 2017

First Published 2017
Reprinted 2019

Donation to Friends of the Elderly
www.fote.org.uk

ISBN 978 1 907598 47 0

Acknowledgements:

The poems in this pamphlet are reprinted from the following books, all by
permission of the publishers listed unless stated otherwise. Every effort has
been made to trace the copyright holders of the poems published in this
book. The editor and publisher apologise if any material has been included
without permission or without the appropriate acknowledgement, and
would be glad to be told of anyone who has not been consulted.

Thanks are due to all the copyright holders cited below for their kind
permission:

Tiffany Atkinson, *Kink and Particle* (Seren, 2006). John Burnside, *Selected
Poems* (Jonathan Cape, 2006). Katie Cleverley, poem as yet unpublished,
by kind permission of the author. Vikki Feaver, *The Book of Blood*
(Jonathan Cape, 2006). Katerina de Jong and Anastasia Matveeva (with
additional Urdu phrases by Minnah Rashid), poem as yet unpublished, by
kind permission of the authors. Joan Johnston, *What You Want* (Diamond
Twig Press, 1999) by permission of the author and publisher. Mohja
Kahf, *E-mails from Scheherazad* (University Press of Florida, 2003) by
permission of University Press of Florida. Derek Mahon, *New Collected
Poems* (The Gallery Press, 2011) by kind permission of the author and
The Gallery Press, Loughcrew, Oldcastle, County Meath, Ireland. Liz
Soar, poem as yet unpublished, by kind permission of the author. Andrew
Waterhouse, *In* (The Rialto, 2000) by permission of the family of Andrew
Waterhouse.

Where poets are no longer living, their dates are given.

Contents

		Page
Introduction	*Liz Soar*	*5*
Recipe for a Grandparent	*Katie Cleverley*	*7*
The Trunk	*Vicki Feaver*	*8-9*
Kisses at the Airport	*Katerina de Jong and Anastasia Matveeva (additional Urdu phrases by Minnah Rashid)*	*10*
Grandfather	*Derek Mahon*	*11*
She's a Game Old Bird	*Liz Soar*	*12-13*
My Grandparents in 1963	*John Burnside*	*14*
Paddling	*Tiffany Atkinson*	*15*
My Grandmother Washes Her Feet in the Sink of the Bathroom at Sears	*Mohja Kahf*	*16-18*
Safe	*Joan Johnston*	*19*
Climbing my Grandfather	*Andrew Waterhouse*	*20*

Introduction

As the parent of a young child, I'm very much aware of how
often grandparents can be taken for granted, so I was delighted
when my Year 7 pupils chose 'Grandparents' as their theme
for an English poetry project. When Di Slaney offered us the
chance to publish a version of it for Candlestick Press, and to
form the editorial team for the full selection of poems, we were
thrilled. The two student poems included in the anthology –
Katie Cleverley's 'Recipe for a Grandparent' and 'Kisses at the
Airport' by Anastasia Matveeva, Katerina de Jong and Minnah
Rashid – capture, in very different ways, a child's attachment
to a grandparent and do so with both wit and style. Many
congratulations indeed to these pupils.

In choosing the remaining poems, we were conscious of our
different individual experiences. Some of the student editors
have grandparents; others don't. Some of their grandparents live
around the corner; others live around the world. We were drawn
to poems which explored the tension between the familiar and
the unknown, whether geographical, cultural or temporal. Even
the closest relationships between grandparent and grandchild
are characterised by both presence and absence: whilst our
grandparents know us for all of our lives, we know them for
only a fraction of theirs. Perhaps it is precisely this distance that
makes their 'old magic', in Joan Johnston's phrase, all the more
compelling.

Liz Soar

Recipe for a Grandparent

A base mixture of age and wisdom,
a teaspoon of clumsiness,
a handful of memories,
a sprinkle of wrinkles; then stir
and chuck in a chequered jumper
just for good measure.

Add a smidgen of forgetfulness
and a teaspoon of laughter.
Make sure you drizzle generosity
so they will go crazy at Christmas.
Pour funniness and mix it in,
till they have you laughing.

They mustn't be embarrassing
when they start dancing,
so throw in some common sense
to fix that problem. Line the tin
with woolly socks and slippers
then bake until warm to the touch.

Katie Cleverley

The Trunk

Like the girl whose curiosity
unloosed all the world's ills
from a box, I wanted to know

what Grandma kept in her trunk:
under a shawl the colours of flame –
orange, gold, mauve – draped

like a sleeping beast on the top;
the bands of black metal
that held everything in.

So one wet afternoon
she opened it up: pulling out
a fox tippet with dangling claws,

a bead-fringed brocade coat;
a bone teething ring
roughened with bite marks;

then bundles of letters
and photographs – Grandpa
who died of pneumonia

caught at a football match,
Jack in a striped rugby shirt
holding a silver cup – everything

she'd kept to remind her
of what was lost. She was kneeling
on the floor, sniffing, wiping

her eyes on her sleeve,
until there was nothing left
except the long white nightdress

she wanted to be laid out in,
and then mothballs
rolling like peppermints.

Vicki Feaver

Kisses at the Airport

As the plane flies in,
I'm jumping up and down,
Waiting to see her smile...

"Ik hou van je, Katje."

Luggage on the rack,
Round and round,
Look, there's her suitcase!

"Prevet moa darogaya, Nastya!"

As I see her face,
Laughter rolls up my throat,
Like waves from the sea she's just crossed.

"Aap kasay ho pyari beti?"

I see ice-creams on the beach,
Tender hands mending my dress,
I feel her lips on my cheek.

"I love you."
"Ik hou van jou."
"Ya tebya lybly."
"Aap bohat achi hai."

Katerina de Jong and Anastasia Matveeva
(additional Urdu phrases by Minnah Rashid)

Grandfather

They brought him in on a stretcher from the world,
Wounded but humorous; and he soon recovered.
Boiler rooms, row upon row of gantries rolled
Away to reveal the landscape of a childhood
Only he can recapture. Even on cold
Mornings he is up at six with a block of wood
Or a box of nails, discreetly up to no good
Or banging round the house like a four-year-old –

Never there when you call. But after dark
You hear his great boots thumping in the hall
And in he comes, as cute as they come. Each night
His shrewd eyes bolt the door and set the clock
Against the future, then his light goes out.
Nothing escapes him; he escapes us all.

Derek Mahon

She's a Game Old Bird

My granny

takes canary sips
from her service-station tea,
jaundiced eyes lantern-bright
as she asks, again,
who the ambulance is for.

is magpie-quick
the nurses say,
fills her knicker drawer
with plasters, rubber gloves,
someone else's dentures.

sticks her beak in other rooms
Look at'em! Lolling!
picks over the injustice
like a pigeon
pecking at its bruised breast.

preens,
her curled fingers
clawing damp strands.
Presently, she says,
I shall ask you to leave.

sings of her cuckoo-child,
sees his father one day in me
and cups my face,
tells me I have nothing
to be sorry for.

lies in a sketch of stillness:
eyes and mouth drawn
pencil-thin.
A sense of
something flown.

Liz Soar

My Grandparents in 1963

They had moved to the centre of things,
rounded and smooth, and closed upon themselves
like mushrooms,

or like the goblins in my books
they tended the fire in the hearth
and spoke in tongues.

A presence that had grown inside the house
they mingled, like moss and lichen, to suggest
the inextricable,

and sat together, bound in tea and starch,
unbending in the long accomplishment
of permanence, of choosing to be still.

John Burnside

Paddling

My grandmother stands on the sea's lip,
a weathered Aphrodite
in an oyster-coloured mac.
Beyond her the egoless blue
flickers with sails.

My father and I hang back.
We expected Sunday clothes,
a sheer drop to a grievous sea,
a scattering as of confetti. Instead
she shucks her shoes and popsocks
and I glimpse her feet for the first time:
pale Victoriana on the packed sand.

It's early March. The water
bites her ankles as she wades
through bladderwrack and flotsam,
lifting her hem above the breathing swell.
She casts his dust on the webbed foam,
watches the teak box fill and sink.
Gulls work the sky like scissors.
A day made for sailing, and his dinghy
gone for a song to a London couple
with three kids and a hatchback.

She turns, and the low sun
strikes her eyes' flint.
There are traces of what might be ash
on her damp shins, but we say nothing.

Tiffany Atkinson

My Grandmother Washes Her Feet in the Sink
of the Bathroom at Sears

My grandmother puts her feet in the sink
  of the bathroom at Sears
to wash them in the ritual washing for prayer,
wudu,
because she has to pray in the store or miss
the mandatory prayer time for Muslims
She does it with great poise, balancing
herself with one plump matronly arm
against the automated hot-air hand dryer,
after having removed her support knee-highs
and laid them aside, folded in thirds,
and given me her purse and her packages to hold
so she can accomplish this august ritual
and get back to the ritual of shopping for housewares

Respectable Sears matrons shake their heads and frown
as they notice what my grandmother is doing,
an affront to American porcelain,
a contamination of American Standards
by something foreign and unhygienic
requiring civic action and possible use of disinfectant spray
They fluster about and flutter their hands and I can see
a clash of civilizations brewing in the Sears bathroom

My grandmother, though she speaks no English,
catches their meaning and her look in the mirror says,
I have washed my feet over Iznik tile in Istanbul
with water from the world's ancient irrigation systems
I have washed my feet in the bathhouses of Damascus
over painted bowls imported from China

among the best families of Aleppo
And if you Americans knew anything
about civilization and cleanliness,
you'd make wider washbasins, anyway
My grandmother knows one culture – the right one,

as do these matrons of the Middle West. For them,
my grandmother might as well have been squatting
in the mud over a rusty tin in vaguely tropical squalor,
Mexican or Middle Eastern, it doesn't matter which,
when she lifts her well-groomed foot and puts it over the edge.
"You can't do that," one of the women protests,
turning to me, "Tell her she can't do that."
"We wash our feet five times a day,"
my grandmother declares hotly in Arabic.
"My feet are cleaner than their sink.
Worried about their sink, are they? I
should worry about my feet!"
My grandmother nudges me, "Go on, tell them."

Standing between the door and the mirror, I can see
at multiple angles, my grandmother and the other shoppers,
all of them decent and goodhearted women, diligent
in cleanliness, grooming and decorum
Even now my grandmother, not to be rushed,
is delicately drying her pumps with tissues from her purse
For my grandmother always wears well-turned pumps
that match her purse, I think in case someone
from one of the best families of Aleppo
should run into her – here, in front of the Kenmore display

I smile at the midwestern women
as if my grandmother has just said something lovely about them
and shrug at my grandmother as if they
had just apologized through me
No one is fooled, but I

hold the door open for everyone
and we all emerge on the sales floor
and lose ourselves in the great common ground
of housewares on markdown.

Mohja Kahf

Safe

Gran had a way with fires,
made coaxing an art
and taught me how kindling
is also a cradle of a word.
One night she let me light it,
using a spill from the brass galleon
and she did old magic,
threw sugar on it.

Later, tucked in, I heard her
setting the table for breakfast,
the trains in the distance.

Joan Johnston

Climbing my Grandfather

I decide to do it free, without a rope or net.
First, the old brogues, dusty and cracked;
an easy scramble onto his trousers,
pushing into the weave, trying to get a grip.
By the overhanging shirt I change
direction, traverse along his belt
to an earth stained hand. The nails
are splintered and give good purchase,
the skin of his finger is smooth and thick
like warm ice. On his arm I discover
the glassy ridge of a scar, place my feet
gently in the old stitches and move on.
At his still firm shoulder, I rest for a while
in the shade, not looking down,
for climbing has its dangers, then pull
myself up the loose skin of his neck
to a smiling mouth to drink among teeth.
Refreshed, I cross the screed cheek,
to stare into his brown eyes, watch a pupil
slowly open and close. Then up over
the forehead, the wrinkles well-spaced
and easy, to his thick hair (soft and white
at this altitude), reaching for the summit,
where gasping for breath I can only lie
watching clouds and birds circle,
feeling his heat, knowing
the slow pulse of his good heart.

Andrew Waterhouse (1958 – 2001)